STURGEON ACTIVITY BOOK

Created by:
G.R.fitch

Some pages inspired by:
The Fraser River Sturgeon Conservation Society
http://www.frasersturgeon.com

Includes:
White Sturgeon Coloring Page ~ Head Maze ~ Crossword
Word Search Traits ~ Green Sturgeon Coloring Page
Word Search Species ~ Find Sturgy ~ Sturgeon Match-Up
Label the Parts ~ Water Match-Up ~ River Maze ~ True or False ~ Trivia
Help the Sturgeon ~ 3D Sturgeon & Rocks Cutout
Mask Cutout ~ Mad Libs

SOLUTIONS PAGES

http://thesturgeonseekers.tripod.com
gm.sturg@gmail.com

WHITE STURGEON
(Acipenser transmontanus)

G.R.fitch 2007

Head Maze

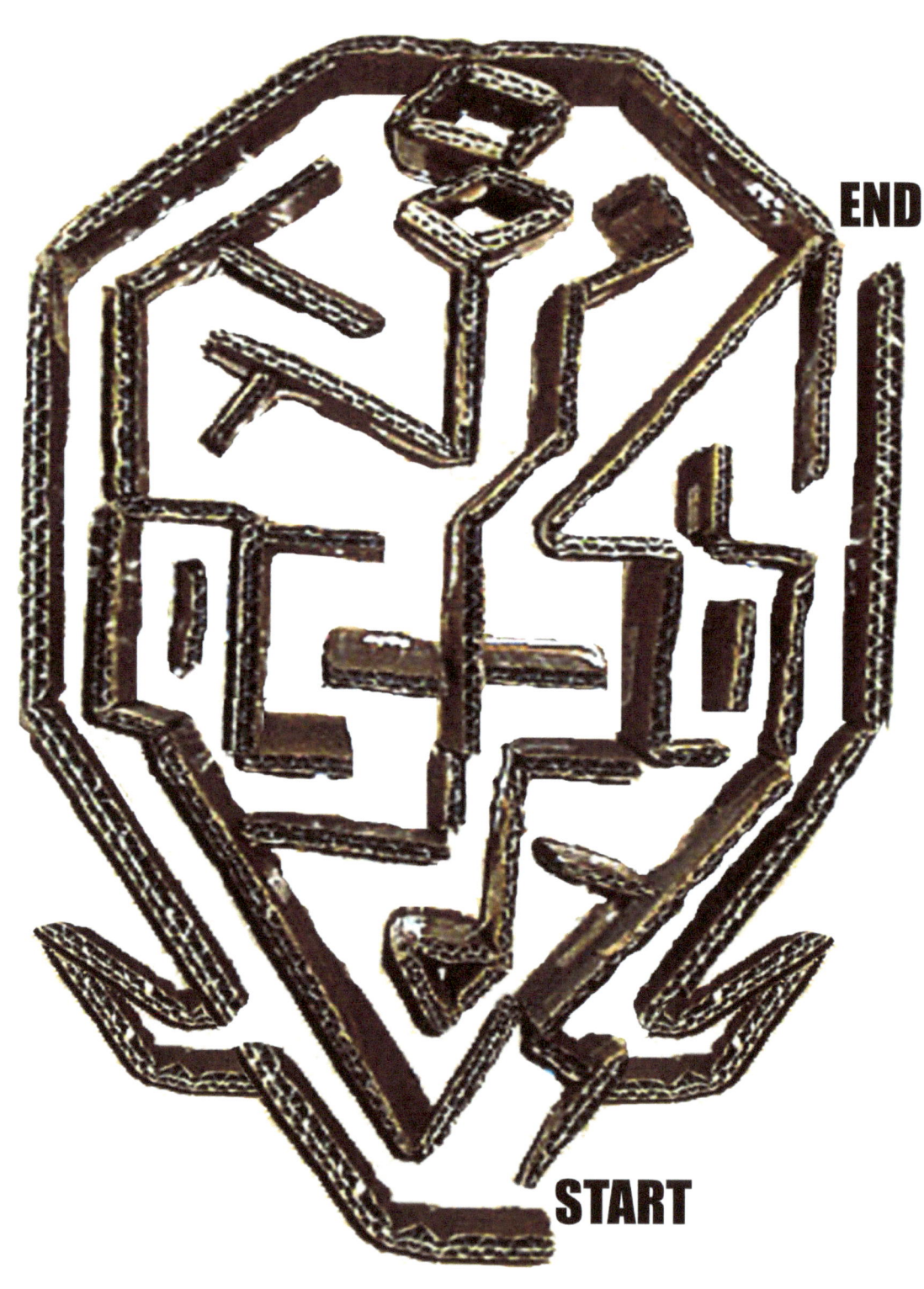

END

START

STURGEON CROSSWORD

ACROSS

1.) Sturgeon do this to spawn.
2.) Swim is this kind of word.
3.) Sturgeon Ball or Party.
4.) Opposite of stop.
5.) Used to eat with.
6.) Harmful Sun Rays. (abv.)
7.) Sturgeon SubFamily.
8.) A Sturgeon who has babies.
9.) Not Swampy but ------.
10.) Sturgeon are a --- fish.
11.) Used to catch fish with.
12.) Slimy Sturgeon food (single)
13.) Opposite of Subtract.
14.) Sturgeon only live here.
15.) Animal Doc. (abv.)
16.) #1 Threat of Sturgeon. (plr.)
17.) Night before the Sturgeon moon.
18.) Black substance on a BBQ.
19.) Salty Lake.
20.) Top fin of a Sturgeon.
21.) Sturgeon are a type of ----.
22.) Scientific name for whiskers.
23.) Do this and release the first fish you catch.
24.) Opposite of False.
25.) Hard-shell food of Sturgeon.
26.) Sturgeon breath with these.
27.) A ------ Aid in finding food.
28.) Caviar Sturgeon
29.) People breath this.

DOWN

1.) Sturgeon can live over this.
2.) To Catch with a Spear.
3.) # of Rows of Scutes.
4.) Sturgeon Ocean Food.
5.) Sturgeon are a -----------.
6.) Country with 9 Sturgeon Species. (abv.)
7.) # of Sturgeon Species
8.) Sturgeon Egg Delicacy.
9.) Crustacean Food of Sturgeon.
10.) Pacific or Atlantic
11.) Nose or -----.
12.) River Block
14.) Smell with this.
15.) Long Body of Fresh Water.
16.) The kind of tail a Sturgeon has.
17.) In the Gills, Removes Food. (plr)
18.) See with (plr)
19.) Bony Plates (plr)
20.) Slimy Sturgeon Predator. (plr)
21.) Sturgeon Food, similar to Sturgeon
22.) Opposite of yes.
23.) Scientific name for most Sturgeon.
24.) Large Body of Fresh Water
25.) Sturgeon Predator, Large Mammal.
26.) Type of Fuel.
27.) What Sturgeon use to swim with. (single)

STURGEON WORDSEARCH
~ TRAITS ETC. ~
Circle the Words, They can be Forward,Backward,& Horizontal

```
H  S  N  D  B  A  R  B  E  L  S  N  I  F  2  8  E
E  U  O  T  D  X  O  O  O  S  A  Q  M  M  9  G  X
T  R  S  B  S  C  U  T  E  S  A  K  N  N  S  Y  T
E  B  T  O  T  X  C  T  C  S  S  W  E  F  P  E  I
R  Y  R  O  U  F  A  O  A  A  D  E  B  B  E  3  N
O  J  I  K  R  R  S  M  S  L  F  R  P  S  C  H  C
C  X  L  R  G  H  R  F  R  G  G  W  R  N  I  T  T
E  D  A  G  E  O  C  E  A  N  H  A  E  O  E  U  D
R  I  C  A  O  I  T  E  T  I  Y  T  H  U  S  O  E
C  N  I  D  N  Q  Y  D  T  S  H  Y  I  T  4  M  R
A  O  P  A  D  D  L  E  F  I  S  H  S  I  F  M  E
L  S  E  D  A  S  U  R  U  F  J  U  T  S  T  U  G
D  A  N  E  P  L  A  T  E  S  K  I  O  R  G  U  N
R  U  S  W  O  R  5  C  A  V  I  A  R  F  I  C  A
S  R  E  K  S  I  H  W  S  R  I  O  I  V  L  A  D
A  I  R  B  L  A  D  D  E  R  L  R  C  B  L  V  N
V  S  U  H  C  N  Y  H  R  I  H  P  A  C  S  D  E
```

BARBEL	GILLS	VACUUMMOUTH
SCUTES	WHISKERS	ISINGLASS
ACIPENSER	HETEROCERCAL	RIVER
HUSO	RAYS	LAKE
CAVIAR	PLATES	OCEAN
PREHISTORIC	SNOUT	SEA
FISH	NOSTRIL	FINS
STURGEON	AIRBLADDER	SCAPHIRHYNCHUS
29SPECIES	DINOSAUR	HUSO
PADDLEFISH	5ROWS	ENDANGERED
WHITE	BOTTOMFEEDER	EXTINCT

GREEN STURGEON
(*Acipenser medirostris*)

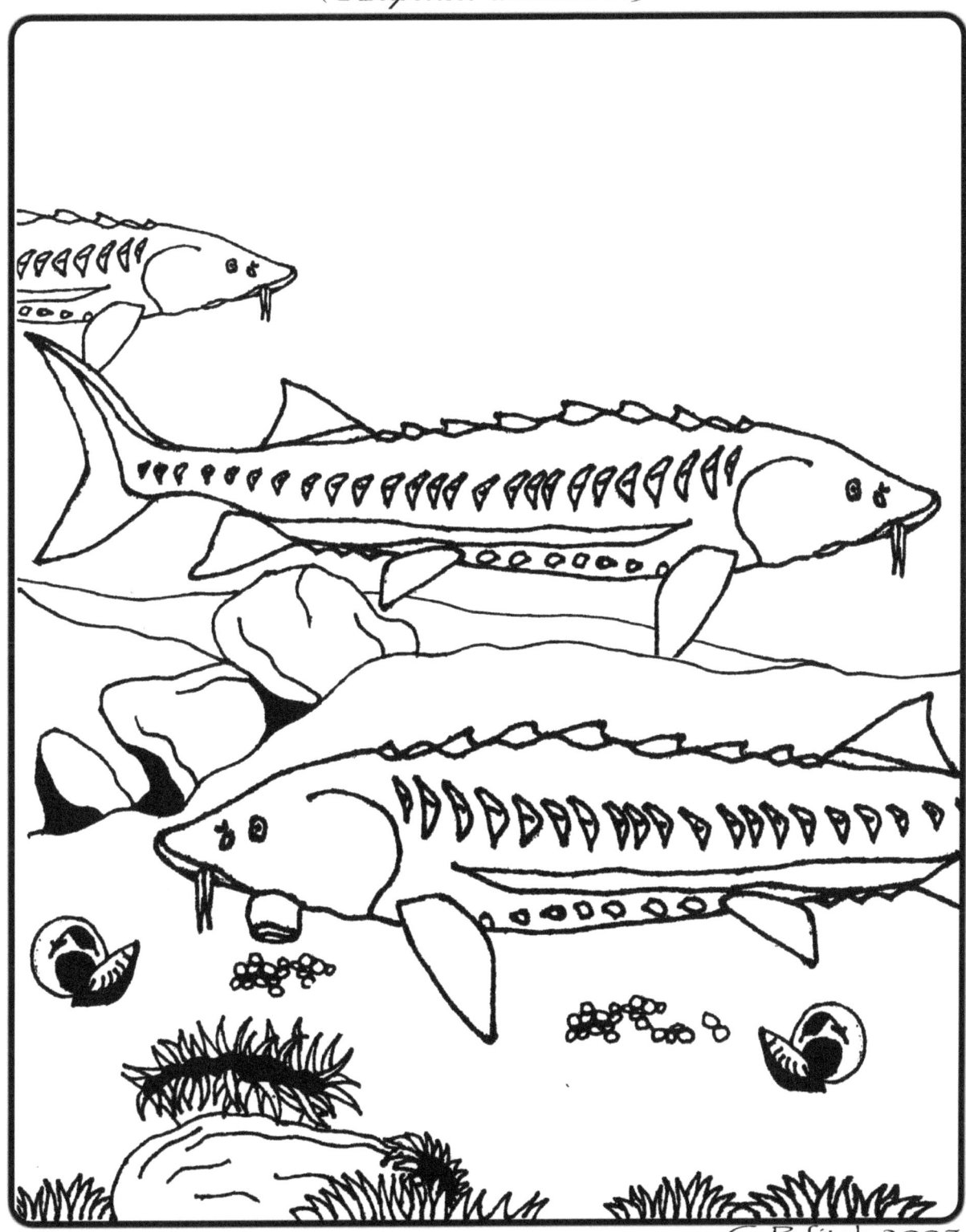

G.R.fitch 2007

STURGEON WORDSEARCH
~ SPECIES ~
Circle the Words, They can be Forward,Backward,& Horizontal

```
A  M  U  R  Z  1  L  E  B  R  A  B  E  G  N  I  R  F
A  A  Q  Z  X  W  A  N  E  D  W  A  E  U  H  H  M  H
Y  A  M  X  E  3  S  I  I  P  H  I  S  L  I  A  O  I
R  S  W  A  R  T  F  L  F  O  A  K  O  F  U  H  R  D
A  D  E  C  B  R  L  A  G  I  N  A  L  W  G  G  E  D
D  F  R  V  T  A  F  H  T  U  O  L  V  G  O  T  A  N
R  G  T  B  P  G  L  K  Y  Y  M  H  T  R  R  Y  T  A
Y  A  N  G  T  Z  E  A  U  T  M  I  E  E  D  D  O  I
S  H  O  R  T  N  O  S  E  S  O  N  L  E  V  O  H  S
I  H  N  N  Y  H  G  T  R  T  C  H  I  N  E  S  E  S
B  J  A  M  U  Y  L  E  N  A  I  I  P  W  E  E  B  U
E  K  I  L  I  T  S  R  P  R  T  A  T  W  K  B  L  R
R  L  S  K  O  E  S  L  O  R  N  I  U  A  T  N  A  M
I  O  R  J  N  B  D  E  I  Y  A  R  L  W  I  M  N  E
A  I  E  A  P  G  F  T  U  T  L  A  Z  W  H  R  K  A
N  T  P  H  8  F  D  I  Y  O  T  M  Z  W  B  D  D  N
K  A  L  U  G  A  G  H  T  T  A  Y  R  A  D  U  M  A
J  R  R  G  F  R  A  W  D  O  T  G  L  W  N  M  U  G
```

ADRIATIC	FRINGEBARBEL	SAKHALIN
ALABAMA	GREEN	SHORTNOSE
AMUDARYA	GULF	SHOVELNOSE
AMUR	JAPANESE	SIBERIAN
ATLANTIC	KALUGA	STARRY
BAIKAL	LAKE	STERLET
BELUGA	LENA	SYRDARYA
CHINESE	PALLID	WHITE
COMMON	PERSIAN	YANGTZE
DWARF	RUSSIAN	

STURGEON MATCH-UP
~ Draw a line from the name to the Sturgeon it goes with ~

Japanese
Gulf
Green
Alabama
Sakhalin
Amur
Fringebarbel
Beluga
Yangtze
Baikal
Chinese
Amy Darya
Adriatic
Common
Lake
Shovelnose
Kaluga
Atlantic
Dwarf
Lena River
Syr Darya
Shortnose
Persian
Siberian
Pallid
White
Sterlet
Starry
Russian

WHITE STURGEON
Acipenser transmontanus

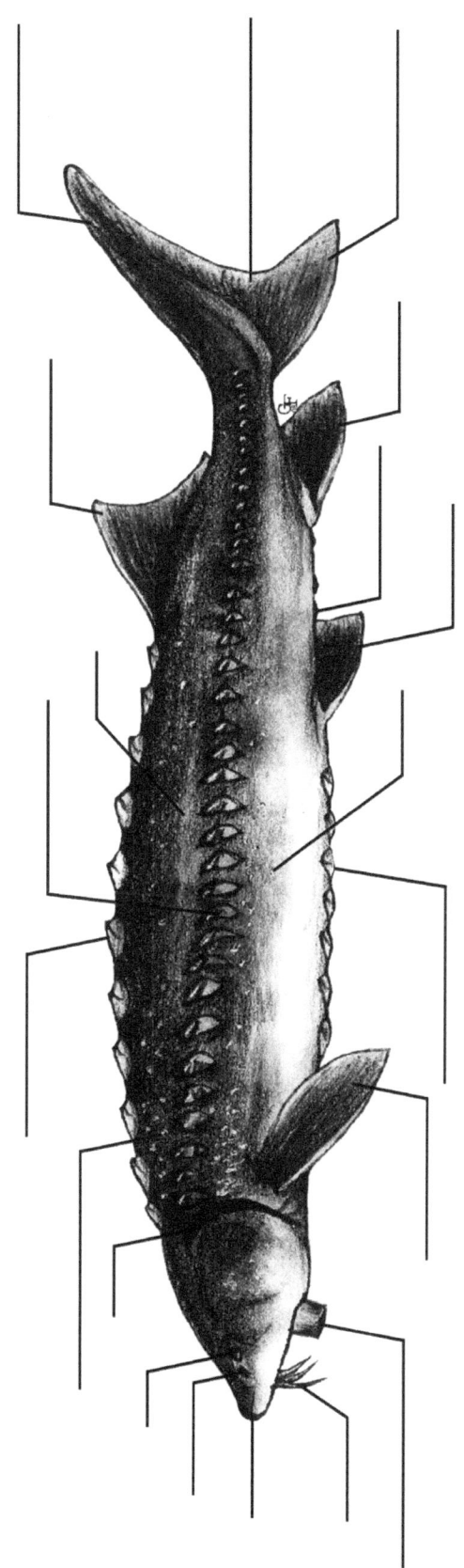

~ Label All The Parts ~

OCEANS, SEAS, LAKES, & RIVERS MATCH-UP
~ Draw a line from the name to the Definition it goes with ~

Lake Baikal	The Shrinking Sea
Atlantic Ocean	Russian Lake
Sacramento River	River bordering OR&WA States
Amur River	North America to Europe Ocean
Great Lakes	Largest Siberian River
Aral Sea	California White Sturgeon River
Columbia River	Italian Adriatic Sturgeon River
Caspian Sea	River bordering Russia & China
Pacific Ocean	North American Lakes
Lena River	River bordering Spain & Portugal
Po River	Worlds Largest Sea
Guadiana River	Oregon Green Sturgeon River
Black Sea	Lake Sturgeon spawning Rivers
Amu Darya River	North America to Asia Ocean
Yangtze River	River bordering Afghan.&Uzbek.
Wolf/Fox Rivers	Canadian White Sturgeon River
Sea of Azov	Large Eurasia Sea
Rogue River	Florida Gulf Sturgeon River
Volga River	Sea of the Black Sea
Ural River	Caspian Sea River in Azerbaijan
Fraser River	Largest Chinese River
Suwannee River	Major spawning Russian River
Danube River	Caspian Sea River in Kazakhstan
Kura River	Sturgeon Rivers of Eastern Canada
Mississippi River	North American Gulf
Rioni River	Black Sea River in Romania
St.John/St.Lawrence	Largest American River
Alabama River	Gulf of Mexico River
Gulf of Mexico	Black Sea River in Georgia

RIVER MAZE

END

START

Help the Gulf Sturgeon get safely through the maze.

STURGEON TRUE or FALSE
~ circle one ~

1.) T or F - Sturgeon can leap completely out of the water.

2.) T or F - Sturgeon have scutes behind the dorsal fin, before the tail.

3.) T or F - Some Sturgeon have scutes before the anal fin.

4.) T or F - Sturgeon can taste with their whiskers/barbels.

5.) T or F - Sturgeon did not live when the Dinosaurs lived.

6.) T or F - Sturgeon can pick up food with their whiskers/barbels.

7.) T or F - The mouth of some Sturgeon can extend out to over 6 inches.

8.) T or F - Sturgeon have an Adipose fin.

9.) T or F - Sturgeon eat Salmon and Salmon eggs.

10.) T or F - Some Sturgeon can weigh up to 4,000 pounds.

11.) T or F - Damming rivers helps Sturgeon.

12.) T or F - Sturgeon have scales.

13.) T or F - Sturgeon have been mentioned in the Guinness Book of World Records.

14.) T or F - The White Sturgeon lives in Russia.

15.) T or F - Sturgeon have a mostly cartilage skeleton.

16.) T or F - Sturgeon have bony plates rather than a skull.

17.) T or F - Sturgeon only live in freshwater.

18.) T or F - Sturgeon live everywhere in the world.

19.) T or F - Sturgeon will eat Sturgeon.

20.) T or F - Sturgeon have sensory pits in their nose/snout.

21.) T or F - The skull and spine of a Sturgeon are bone.

22.) T or F - The smallest Sturgeon only grows up to 9 inches.

23.) T or F - Sturgeon can live out of water for more than 1 day.

24.) T or F - Sturgeon skin has been made into baskets.

25.) T or F - Sturgeon have teeth for up to one year of age.

26.) T or F - Sturgeon scutes can be razor sharp and easily cut flesh.

27.) T or F - Sturgeon build nests in the rocks/gravel to lay their eggs in.

28.) T or F - Sturgeon are slow to recover from illness,injury,harm,misfortune, and stress.

29.) T or F - No Sturgeon species have spikes on their nose.

30.) T or F - Sturgeon eggs hatch in 30 days.

31.) T or F - Sturgeon have to die for their eggs to be used for caviar.

32.) T or F - Sturgeon live over 200 years.

33.) T or F - All species of Sturgeon are the same color.

34.) T or F - All species of Sturgeon are raised in hatcheries.

35.) T or F - Sturgeon only live in Salt water.

36.) T or F - Sturgeon have 6 Barbels/Whiskers.

37.) T or F - All Sturgeon are endangered.

38.) T or F - Sturgeon were completely utilized by native peoples of the world.

39.) T or F - There are no festivals for/about Sturgeon.

40.) T or F - Sturgeon eat people.

STURGEON TRIVIA

1.) Scientific name for most Sturgeon._____

2.) Tactile organs near the mouth. _____

3.) Bony plates. _____

4.) A mix of salt & fresh water. _____

5.) Sturgeon have a _____ tail. Where the top is longer than the bottom.

6.) Sturgeon live in these four bodies of water _____,_____,_____,_____

7.) Largest Sturgeon species. _____

8.) Sturgeon eggs delicacy. _____

9.) Extracts oxygen from the water. _____

10.) Number of rows of scutes. _____

11.) The shrinking sea. _____

12.) Number of Asian Sturgeon. _____

13.) Most threatened or possibly extinct Sturgeon. _____

14.) Some Sturgeon can live over _____ years.

15.) Scientific name for Beluga Sturgeon. _____

16.) Closest Sturgeon relative. _____ and/or _____

17.) The month of the Sturgeon Moon. _____

18.) Sturgeon have a _____ mouth.

19.) Number of recognized Sturgeon species. _____

20.) Smallest Sturgeon. _____

21.) Sturgeon live only in the _____ Hemisphere.

22.) Number of European Sturgeon species. _____

23.) #1 Threat of All Sturgeon _____

24.) Number of Sturgeon species in North America _____

25.) Several Sturgeon species can grow to over _____ feet.

26.) Baby Sturgeon are called. _____

27.) Number of Eurasian/Central Asia Sturgeon species. _____

28.) The Journey Sturgeon make to spawn. _____

29.) Some Sturgeon can lay over _____ eggs.

30.) Number of Russian Sturgeon species. _____

31.) A Sturgeon predator that attaches to the Sturgeon to feed. _____

32.) River wall/block that is a major threat to Sturgeon. _____

33.) Sturgeon have a _____ stomach.

34.) Sturgeon are this kind of feeder. _____

35.) Large mammal that is a Sturgeon predator. _____

36.) Sturgeon are a _____ fish.

37.) Sturgeon have lived basically unchanged for _____ million years.

38.) Most Sturgeon eggs hatch in _____ days.

39.) Sturgeon are an _____ fish, that migrate from the ocean/sea to spawn in fresh water.

40.) Sturgeon have existed for over _____ years.

WAYS TO HELP THE STURGEON

~ Answer these questions with anything you can think of - possible answers in the back ~

What are 5 things everyone can do to help Sturgeon?
1.)_____
2.)_____
3.)_____
4.)_____
5.)_____

Name 5 Sturgeon Related Occupations.
1.)_____
2.)_____
3.)_____
4.)_____
5.)_____

What are 5 ways to help the waters that Sturgeon live in?
1.)_____
2.)_____
3.)_____
4.)_____
5.)_____

What are 5 helpful things to do while fishing for Sturgeon?
1.)_____
2.)_____
3.)_____
4.)_____
5.)_____

3-D WHITE STURGEON CUTOUT DISPLAY

1.) CAREFULLY CUT OUT AROUND STURGEON, BE CAREFUL CUTTING ARROW.
2.) FOLD IN HALF
3.) CUT AT LINES TO CUT OUT INSIDE SECTIONS
4.) CAREFULLY CUT OUT INSIDE SECTIONS, BE CAREFUL CUTTING ARROW.
5.) BEND ARROWS OUT/OVER ON OUTSIDE OF STURGEON AND INSERT INTO PRE-CUT SLITS
6.) BEND THE FIRST AND SECOND FINS UP SLIGHTLY
7.) SET OVER ROCKS

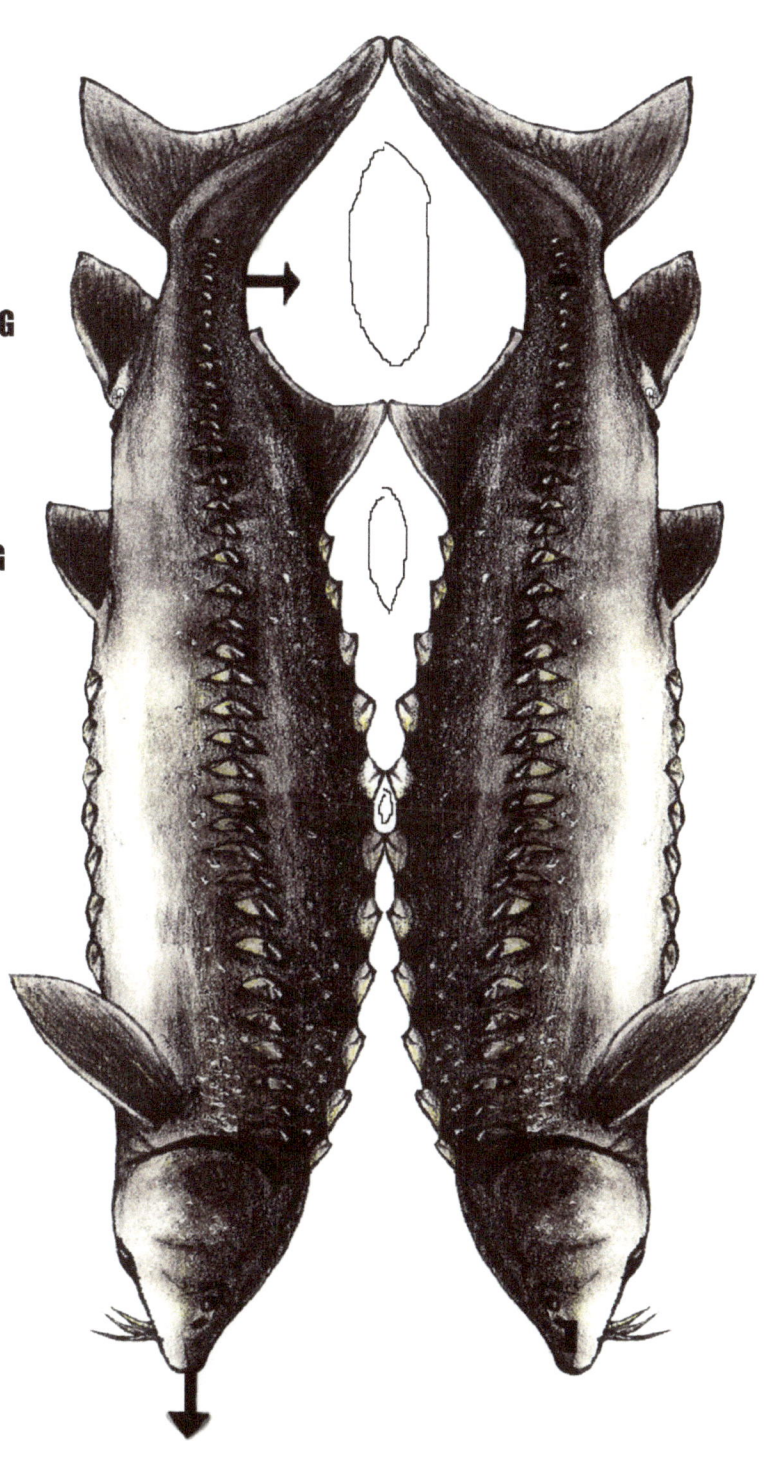

3-D WHITE STURGEON CUTOUT DISPLAY

CUT SLIT

FOLD HERE

FOLD HERE

CUT SLIT

FOLD HERE

FOLD HERE

CUT SLIT

CUT SLIT

1.) CUT ALONG LINES/CUT OUT SIDES
2.) FOLD IN HALF
3.) FOLD AT (FOLD HERE) SPOTS
4.) CUT BLACK SLIT LINES
5.) CUT OUT ROCKS
6.) FIT SLITS TOGETHER
7.) BEND SLIT AREAS/TABS BACK SHOWING ROCK
8.) SET STURGEON ON TOP

Sturgeon Head Mask

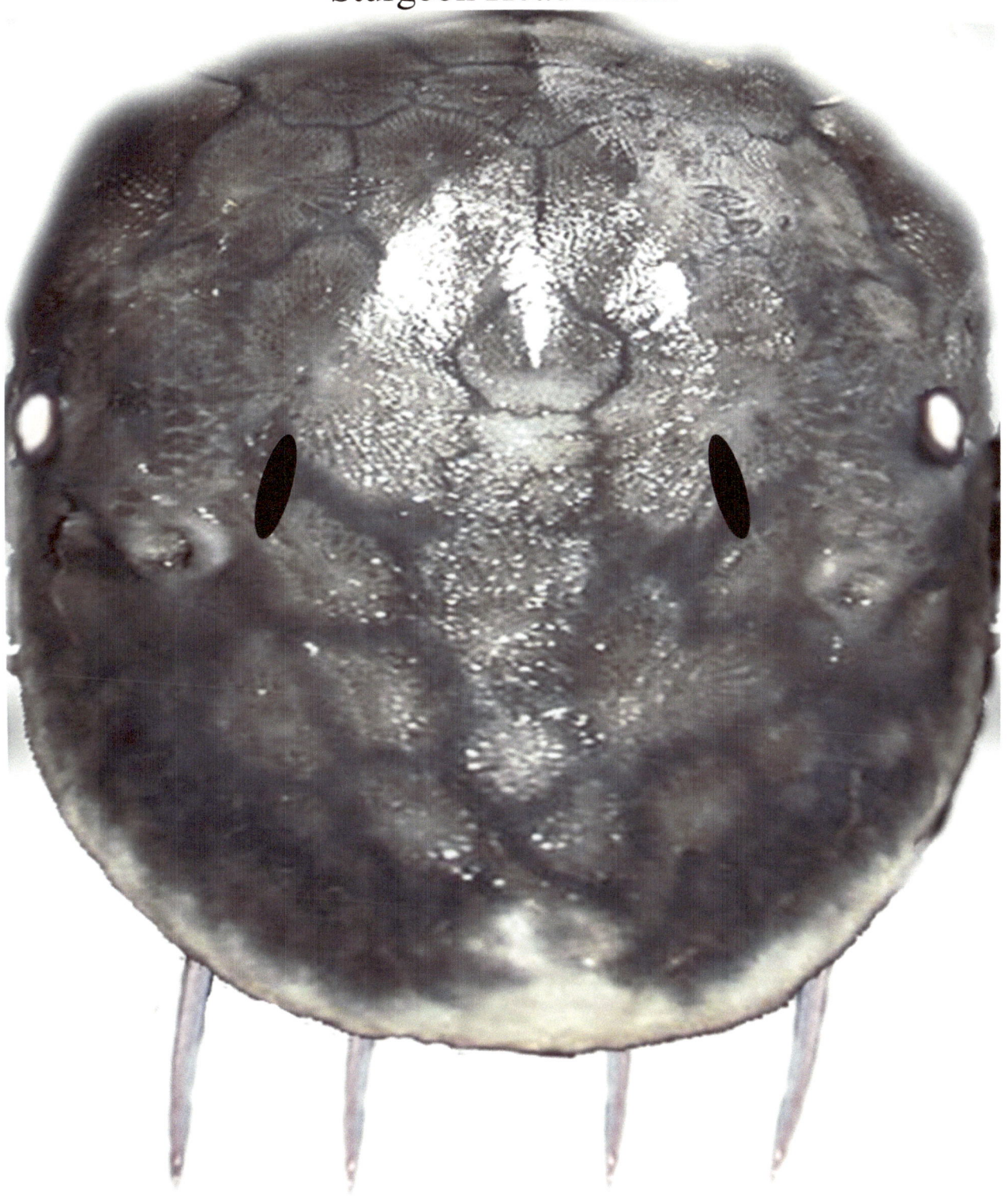

Carefully cut-out around edges and cut-out Black Ovals for eyes. Careful not to cut the elastic thread.

STURGEON MAD LIBS
~ Fill in the space with the suggested kind of word ~
~ Use a pencil for multiple uses ~

Sturgeon Journey

The Sturgeon _____ in the river searching for _____.
                 (verb)   *(noun)*

It found a _____ fish and _____ it.
           (adjective)   *(verb)*

Later, the _____ Sturgeon _____ to the estuary to
           (adjective)   *(verb)*

Meet up with the other _____ Sturgeon. Together they all
                       (adjective)

_____ up the _____ to go to the spawning
    (verb)   *(noun)*

_____ to _____.
  (plural noun)   *(verb)*

Strange Fish

Sturgeon are very _____ _____. They have existed
               (adjective)   *(noun)*

for _____ years. They were alive when the _____
    (number)   *(plural noun)*

were alive. And Sturgeon have _____ basically unchanged for
                     (past tense verb)

_____ years. So, Sturgeon are a/an _____ fish that
  (number)   *(adjective)*

look very _____ but many _____ think they look
       (adjective)   *(plural noun)*

_____.
  (adjective)

SOLUTIONS PAGE 1

HEAD MAZE SOLUTION

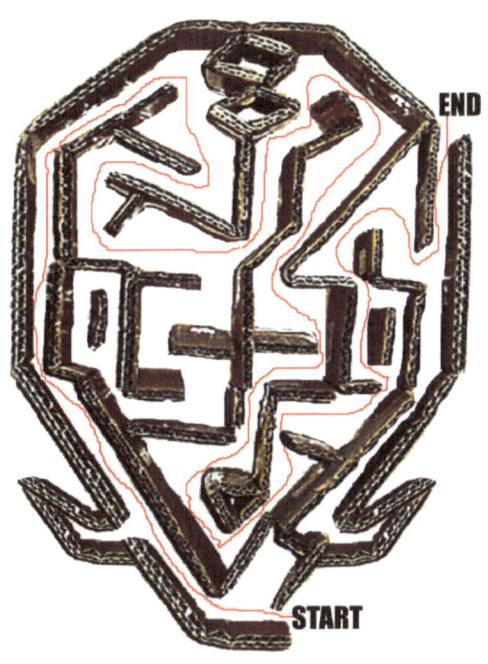

CROSSWORD SOLUTION

WORDSEARCH TRAITS SOLUTION

WORDSEARCH SPECIES SOLUTION

SOLUTIONS PAGE 2

FIND STURGYS SOLUTION

STURGEON MATCH-UP SOLUTION

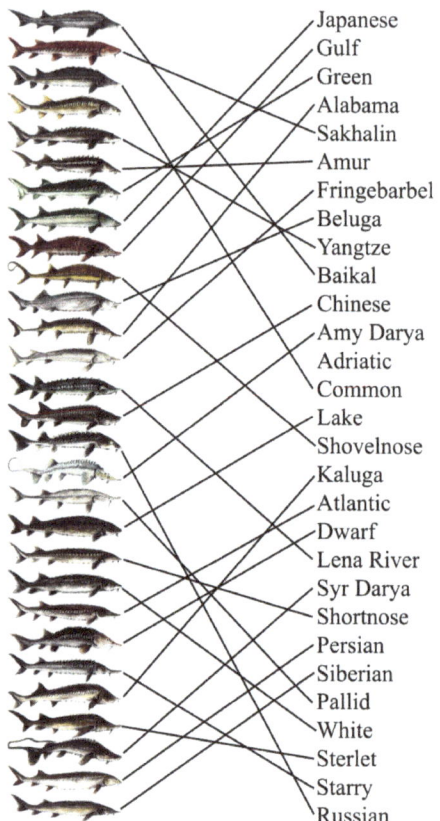

Japanese
Gulf
Green
Alabama
Sakhalin
Amur
Fringebarbel
Beluga
Yangtze
Baikal
Chinese
Amy Darya
Adriatic
Common
Lake
Shovelnose
Kaluga
Atlantic
Dwarf
Lena River
Syr Darya
Shortnose
Persian
Siberian
Pallid
White
Sterlet
Starry
Russian

LABEL PARTS SOLUTION

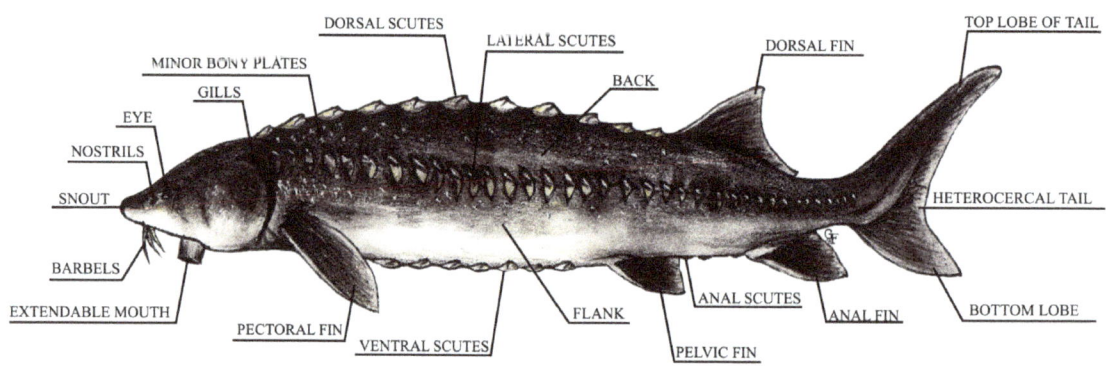

SOLUTIONS PAGE 3

WATER MATCH-UP SOLUTION

Lake Baikal	The Shrinking Sea
Atlantic Ocean	Russian Lake
Sacramento River	River bordering OR&WA States
Amur River	North America to Europe Ocean
Great Lakes	Largest Siberian River
Aral Sea	California White Sturgeon River
Columbia River	Italian Adriatic Sturgeon River
Caspian Sea	River bordering Russia & China
Pacific Ocean	North American Lakes
Lena River	River bordering Spain & Portugal
Po River	Worlds Largest Sea
Guadiana River	Oregon Green Sturgeon River
Black Sea	Lake Sturgeon spawning Rivers
Amu Darya River	North America to Asia Ocean
Yangtze River	River bordering Afghan.&Uzbek.
Wolf/Fox Rivers	Canadian White Sturgeon River
Sea of Azov	Large Eurasia Sea
Rogue River	Florida Gulf Sturgeon River
Volga River	Sea of the Black Sea
Ural River	Caspian Sea River in Azerbaijan
Fraser River	Largest Chinese River
Suwannee River	Major spawning Russian River
Danube River	Caspian Sea River in Kazakhstan
Kura River	Sturgeon Rivers of Eastern Canada
Mississippi River	North American Gulf
Rioni River	Black Sea River in Romania
St.John/St.Lawrence	Largest American River
Alabama River	Gulf of Mexico River
Gulf of Mexico	Black Sea River in Georgia

RIVER MAZE SOLUTION

STURGEON TRUE or FALSE
~ ANSWERS ~

1.) **T** or F - The White and Gulf Sturgeon are known to leap out of the water.

2.) T or **F** - Sturgeon <u>do not</u> have scutes behind the dorsal fin, before the tail.

3.) T or F - Some Sturgeon do have scutes before the anal fin, and even 2 rows.

4.) **T** or F - Sturgeon can taste with their whiskers/barbels which house taste buds.

5.) T or **F** - Sturgeon <u>did</u> live when the Dinosaurs lived.

6.) T or **F** - Sturgeon <u>can not</u> pick up food with their whiskers/barbels.

7.) **T** or F - The mouth of some Sturgeon can extend out to over 6 inches.

8.) T or **F** - Sturgeon <u>do not</u> have an Adipose fin, only a Doral fin.

9.) **T** or F - Sturgeon do eat Salmon carcasses and Salmon eggs.

10.) **T** or F - Some Sturgeon can weigh up to 4,000 pounds, such as the Beluga.

11.) T or **F** - Damming rivers <u>harms</u> Sturgeon mainly by blocking their spawning grounds

12.) T or **F** - Sturgeon <u>do not</u> have scales but many have lots of little bony plates.

13.) **T** or F - The Beluga was in the G. B. of W. R. as the most expensive fish for caviar.

14.) T or **F** - The White Sturgeon only lives off the Pacific Ocean in North America.

15.) **T** or F - Sturgeon have a mostly cartilage skeleton.

16.) **T** or F - Sturgeon have bony plates rather than a skull.

17.) T or **F** - Some Sturgeon only live in freshwater but not all of them.

18.) T or **F** - Sturgeon only live in the Northern Hemisphere.

19.) **T** or F - Sturgeon are cannibals and will eat other Sturgeon.

20.) **T** or F - Sturgeon have sensory pits in their nose/snout.

21.) T or **F** - The skull and spine of a Sturgeon are not bone they are cartilage.

22.) **T** or F - The smallest Sturgeon, the Dwarf Sturgeon, only grows up to 9 inches.

23.) T or **F** - Sturgeon can possibly live for hours out of water but not more than 1 day.

24.) **T** or F - Sturgeon skin has been made into baskets by a Seattle Wa. artist.

25.) **T** or F - Sturgeon have 2 fang-like teeth for up to one year of age.

26.) **T** or F - Sturgeon scutes can be razor sharp and easily cut flesh.

27.) T or **F** - Sturgeon are egg scatterers and do not build nests.

28.) **T** or F - Sturgeon have a very low to medium Resiliency.

29.) T or **F** - The Amu Darya Sturgeon does have 1-2 pairs of spikes on their nose.

30.) T or **F** - Sturgeon eggs usually hatch at around 10 days.

31.) **T** or F - Sturgeon <u>do</u> have to die for their eggs to be used for caviar.

32.) T or **F** - Sturgeon <u>do not</u> live over 200 years but 5 can live up to or over 100 years.

33.) T or **F** - All species of Sturgeon are <u>not</u> the same color and can vary greatly.

34.) T or **F** - Most species of Sturgeon are raised in hatcheries but not all.

35.) T or **F** - Sturgeon <u>do not</u> only live in Salt water.

36.) T or **F** - Sturgeon <u>do not</u> have 6 Barbels/Whiskers they have 4. Some have 2 pairs.

37.) **T** or F - All Sturgeon are endangered and are vulnerable to extinction.

38.) **T** or F - Sturgeon were completely utilized by native peoples of the world.

39.) T or **F** - There <u>are</u> festivals for/about Sturgeon all over the world.

40.) **T** or F - Sturgeon will eat the carcass of a human in the water.

TRIVIA ANSWERS

1.) Acipenser
2.) Barbels/Whiskers
3.) Scutes
4.) Brackish
5.) Heterocercal
6.) Ocean, Sea, Lake, River
7.) Beluga
8.) Caviar
9.) Gills
10.) 5
11.) Aral Sea
12.) 6
13.) Alabama
14.) 100
15.) Huso Huso
16.) Mississippi Paddlefish, Chinese Swordfish
17.) August
18.) Protractile, Vacuum, Suction, Extendable
19.) 29
20.) Dwarf
21.) Northern
22.) 9
23.) Man, People, Humans, Us, We Are
24.) 9
25.) 20
26.) Larval, Larvae
27.) 8
28.) Migration
29.) 400,000
30.) 12
31.) Eel, Lamprey Eel
32.) Dam
33.) Gizzard Like
34.) Bottom
35.) Seal, Sea Lion
36.) Prehistoric
37.) 65
38.) 10
39.) Anadromous
40.) 150 million

WAYS TO HELP THE STURGEON
~ Some Possible Answers ~

<u>What are 5 things everyone can do to help Sturgeon?</u>
1.) Recycle
2.) Use less water
3.) Drive less, Use fuel efficient cars, ride a bike
4.) Be educated about Sturgeon
5.) Buy Sturgeon merchandise
6.) Don't fish for Sturgeon, or Catch & Release
7.) Live Green, Use Green/Earth friendly products
8.) Support Aquariums, Hatcheries, Zoos, Universities
9.) Be a member of Sturgeon organizations such as World Sturgeon Conservation Society, Sturgeon for Tomorrow, International Centre for Sturgeon Studies, etc.

<u>Name 5 Sturgeon Related Occupations.</u>
1.) Biologist
2.) Hatchery Worker/Owner
3.) Aquarium Worker
4.) Fisherman/Guide
5.) Sturgeon Artist
6.) Activist
7.) Naturalist
8.) Environmentalist
9.) Teacher/Professor/Instructor
10.) Zoo Worker

<u>What are 5 ways to help the waters that Sturgeon live in?</u>
1.) Remove dams/Open channels in dams/Don't dam rivers
2.) Reduce (don't use) pollutants/fertilizers/industrial waste, runoff
3.) Use less water
4.) Plant trees/bushes to reduce water runoff/erosion
5.) Clean the shores/Pick up trash and human debris/Don't litter
6.) Recycle
7.) Stop oil drilling
8.) Limit/Stop fishing
9.) Live Green.

<u>What are 5 helpful things to do while fishing for Sturgeon?</u>
1.) Use heavier line than you think you will need
2.) Use barbless hooks
3.) Bring the fish in fast/Don't "Play" the fish
4.) Fish from a boat
5.) Release the fish fast & carefully
6.) Don't take the fish completely out of the water.
7.) Catch & Release/Don't kill the fish/Don't keep the fish.
8.) Use lead free weights
9.) Use a heavier pole than necessary
10.) Don't fish for Sturgeon